Original title:
The Call of the Island

Copyright © 2025 Creative Arts Management OÜ
All rights reserved.

Author: Nolan Kingsley
ISBN HARDBACK: 978-1-80581-537-2
ISBN PAPERBACK: 978-1-80581-064-3
ISBN EBOOK: 978-1-80581-537-2

Horizons Chasing Shadows

Waves giggle as they nudge the shore,
Seagulls squawk like they're keeping score.
Tanned tourists with oversized hats,
Mistaken for jellybeans or chubby cats.

Coconuts rolling like they're in a race,
Sandcastles topple with minimal grace.
Flip-flops flapping, never a care,
Like marching bands made of sun and air.

The Dance of Dunes

The sands twist and swirl, a calypso cheer,
Even the lizards join in the steer.
Turtles boogie, with an awkward shimmy,
Flopping and sliding, oh so dizzy!

A crab with a top hat struts on by,
While the breeze plays notes that make you sigh.
Giggling fish, in a shimmering swirl,
The ocean's combined with a giddy whirl.

Yearning for Bright Horizons

Palm trees sway like they're in a trance,
While sunburnt folks try to find romance.
Ice cream cones dribble, a sticky mess,
It's hard to flirt when your shirt's a stress!

The beach ball bounces, a cheerful sphere,
Chasing toddlers who elude with cheer.
Splashing and laughing, umbrellas upside down,
A spectacle worthy of any clown!

The Night's Invitation

Under starlit skies, the crickets sing,
While jellyfish float with a glow like bling.
Dancing shadows play peek-a-boo,
As everyone waits for the moon's debut.

Coconut drinks clink with a cheers and a cheers,
As everyone shares their wildest fears.
Octopuses juggle, a sight to behold,
In the hilarious night, stories unfold!

Tides that Shape Our Journeys

Waves giggle as they dance along,
Tickling toes with a playful song.
Seagulls swoop, they tease and dive,
While surfers try to look alive.

Buckets full of shells and sand,
The castle's leaning—who made this land?
Kids running, laughter fills the air,
As crabs scuttle, without a care.

Nature's Symphony in Azure Waters

Shells clattering like a funky band,
Fish flipping, trying to make a stand.
The wind plays tricks with hats that fly,
While dolphins wave, saying hi!

Palm trees dance with a cheeky sway,
Offering shade for a lazy stay.
Picnic spreads, ants join the feast,
As laughter echoes, never ceased.

Uncharted Realms of Ocean Blue

A pirate's life, says one brave soul,
But his map just leads to a picnic role.
Detours taken with no regrets,
As we sail into snack attack quests.

Underwater treasures not far below,
Floaties bounce like a rodeo.
Swimmers splash like silly seals,
While the sun beams down, and laughter feels.

Footprints in the Salted Breeze

Leaving marks like a clumsy dance,
As seagulls watch and glance askance.
Sand stuck where it just won't budge,
While shells whisper, 'Oh, you just judge!'

Chasing waves like a game of tag,
While sunscreen lotions leak and sag.
The horizon beckons, a friendly tease,
With salty winds that say, 'Just freeze!'

Siren Songs of Lost Adventures

In the beach chairs, we sit and sway,
Counting crabs that dance away.
The seagulls mock with squawking cheer,
As sunburns spread from ear to ear.

We dug for treasure, found a shoe,
A starfish smiled, oh what a view!
With every splash, we let out a shriek,
The ocean's treasure—mystique and geek.

Sanctuaries of Solitude and Sand

On a sandy throne, I reign supreme,
While ants debate, they plot and scheme.
My coconut cup spills its sweet drink,
The seagulls laugh, they know what I think.

Hours lost to sun and surf,
I'll trade my worries for a mermaid birth.
Each wave that crashes brings a tease,
I laugh aloud, oh, this life's a breeze!

Dreaming in Tropical Breezes

Pineapples sway in the marketplace,
While tourists dance with clumsy grace.
A hammock's lull begs dreams to play,
As I snooze and drift, come what may.

Mango sticky on my sun-kissed face,
I waltz with a crab that picks up the pace.
Forgotten worries float like driftwood,
In this paradise, life feels so good.

Dance of the Waves and Shadows

The waves are high, the shadows play,
I've lost my towel, hey, what a day!
The flip-flops float like little boats,
While dolphins tease with splashes and jotes.

My portable grill sends smoke on a spree,
As beachgoers search for a better berry.
With laughter ringing through the sunlit air,
We dance like fish, without a care!

Embrace of Salt and Sun

Sandy toes and clammy hands,
Ice cream drips on the hot dry sands.
Seagulls squawk, they steal my fries,
Laughter echoes under bright blue skies.

Buckets filled with dreams and shells,
Dancing crabs, they ring their bells.
Flip-flops flying in the breeze,
Who knew sunburns could bring such ease?

Lavenders in a Coastal Breeze

Lavender blooms and salty spray,
A windmill spins in a clumsy way.
Beach balls bounce, oh what a sight,
Sunburned noses and laughter ignite.

Flip-flops flip as seagulls dive,
Pinch my cheeks, I feel alive!
Sandcastles rise, then fall like dreams,
With frosting waves and whipped cream seams.

The Rhythm of Lapping Waves

Waves wash in, then out they go,
Splashing at my toes, quite the show.
Belly flops and sandy falls,
Giggles sound like waterfall calls.

Jellyfish dance like balloons afloat,
In a sea of fun, we all gloat.
Sunset paints the sky with cheer,
As I drop my sandwich in the pier.

Unwritten Stories of the Sea

A pirate's hat, on my brother's head,
He swabs the deck, but ends up red.
Mermaids chime in shimmering scales,
While fish discuss our silly tales.

Seashell secrets and jelly bean dreams,
Waves giggle softly, or so it seems.
Lighthouses wink as the sun dips low,
Time for ice cream, let the good times flow!

From Promises to Parchment

A pirate found a treasure map,
With ink that smudged and dripped like sap.
He followed lines on paper gold,
But found instead a fruit stand bold.

With mangoes, pineapples, and some lime,
He traded all his dreams for time.
For riches bought with laughter's grain,
Feasts of joy, and no more pain.

The Language of Seagrass

The seagrass whispered secrets low,
Of fishy gossip and more to show.
A crab with sass and a clam with flair,
Held court beneath the ocean's stare.

They spoke of tides and seashell wars,
Of who could dance on sandy shores.
With flippers 'n fins they took their flight,
In underwater limelight, oh what a sight!

Forgotten Legends of the Sea

Old tales of mermaids with glittery tails,
Now sing in the breeze, like fishy gales.
A tuna dressed as a dapper gent,
Claimed he'd teach whales that he could lent.

They danced and swam through currents wild,
With jellyfish glowing like a child.
But legends fade in salty air,
Leave us laughing, unaware of a scare.

Glistening Shores of Solitude

On shores so bright, the crabs congregate,
Each sporting a hat, oh isn't that great?
They gossip about the fish in the sea,
Unbothered by waves, wild and free.

A lone seagull watches in delight,
As they stage a show, oh what a sight!
With each peck, a punchline's shared anew,
Glistening moments that they construe.

Navigating Untamed Waters

On a boat made of bubble gum,
We sail where the jellyfish hum.
Riding waves on a surfboard made of cheese,
Losin' our hats to the playful breeze.

Seagulls squawking like they own the place,
Chasing them down for a quick embrace.
Our map is a pizza, cut just so,
And we're lost 'cause the crust won't go slow.

Crabs doing the cha-cha on the shore,
While we try to dance, oh what a chore!
We trip over shells and laugh till we cry,
As the sunset winks its sleepy eye.

Secrets of the Distant Horizon

There's treasure out here, or so they say,
Hidden just beyond the flaming bay.
We brought our spoons instead of a spade,
To dig for bananas in the shade.

Palm trees whisper like they're sharing tricks,
While we hunt for gold that's really just bricks.
The horizon giggles, as we scratch our heads,
Off the beaten path, in our pirate dreads.

A map with crayons is our leading clue,
Pointing to places where the coconuts grew.
But all we find are old flip-flops and glee,
As we paint the sky with our wild monkey spree.

In the Embrace of the Mist

The fog rolls in like a fluffy pet cat,
Hiding our ship and the old fisherman's hat.
We toss out our nets but catch only air,
And the fish all giggle, 'We're not even there!'

Waves are laughing, a joke we don't get,
Stumbling through mist like a quirky duet.
Whispers of sea turtles float in the breeze,
Telling us tales with the greatest of ease.

Bubbles pop loudly, a chorus of fun,
As we trip over jelly, oh what a run!
In this playful dance with the ocean and sky,
We'll remember this adventure as the days flutter by.

Tide Pools of Memory

In a tide pool, we just found a sock,
Said it belonged to a very lost rock.
The creatures inside are putting on a show,
While we take notes like we're in a zoo, you know?

A starfish is winking, it's made of pure sass,
Telling us stories while we laugh and gasp.
Seaweed is tickling our toes as we stare,
At the crabs doing cartwheels without a care.

The wise old mollusk drops wisdom like pearls,
While we try to catch fish in our bright twirls.
Our memories splashed with the sea's amiable grace,
Are treasures we gather in this bubbly place!

The Petals of Distant Shores

On sandy banks where coconuts sway,
The crabs throw a party every day.
They dance in circles, a lively team,
While seagulls plot their latest scheme.

A parrot mocks the sailor's shout,
As fish wear hats and swim about.
The waves tickle toes, the sun's a friend,
In this wacky world, where laughter won't end.

Flip-flops fly as folks chase the tide,
With rubber duckies flapping in pride.
Each splash and giggle paints joy's embrace,
In a beachside circus, life's a race.

So grab a drink with a tiny straw,
And take in the antics of this grand law.
For in every giggle, every playful pain,
Life's a weird carnival by the main.

Remnants of Seafarers

Upon a wreck, where barnacles cling,
The ghost of a sailor starts to sing.
His tune is wobbly, like a fish on land,
With seaweed dancers, they make a band.

The compass spins, it's lost its way,
It points to snacks on this fine day.
A treasure chest spills not gold or pearls,
But rubber ducks and old, soggy swirls.

Fish in tuxedos form a parade,
Waving to crabs with plans well laid.
Bottles bob while whispers ignite,
"Who's bringing the chips for tonight's bite?"

So raise a toast with coconut milk,
In this merry mess, smooth as silk.
For every scrap from waves that roamed,
Is a reminder that merriment's home.

Untold Tales of the Drift

A seaweed monster with googly eyes,
Tells tall tales that cause much surprise.
He speaks of pirates at breakfast time,
With stories so silly they seem like a rhyme.

Old shoes collect as treasures unfold,
Shiny and strange—worth more than gold.
Each floaty critter, each flotsam plea,
Sings of adventures, wild and free.

They spin their yarns by the gulf's soft breeze,
Of daring escapes and slipping knees.
A dolphin quips, "That wave was a fright!"
As gulls squawk laughter, oh what a sight!

So gather round as the dusk brings cheer,
For mysteries swirl with the ocean's leer.
Beneath the starlight, let's quirk and drift,
In the realm of tales that the tides do lift.

Serpentine Paths by Moonlit Waters

Down winding trails by the shimmering light,
Squirrels in goggles take daring flight.
With every leap, they giggle and scream,
In a moonlit race that feels like a dream.

The fish wear wigs, and the frogs sport crowns,
As shadows dance in the silvery downs.
Each ripple in water holds secrets to share,
Of splashy mischief in the cool night air.

A turtle rides waves on a floaty bright,
While crickets compose a symphony tonight.
The laughter echoes, resounding wide,
In this zany world where antics abide.

So follow the paths where fun is the rule,
And let your heart be a jolly fool.
For in these waters, under the sky,
Every moment's magic — oh me, oh my!

Embrace of the Ocean Breeze

The coconut fell with a thump,
A seagull squawked, doing the jump.
"Don't eat my sandwich!" I cried out loud,
While crabs danced merrily, gathering a crowd.

The waves laughed, splashing my toes,
As seaweed tangled in my nose.
"Is that a fish or just a shoe?"
I pondered aloud, the ocean's quite the zoo.

The sun wore shades, a silly display,
While dolphins flipped, crazy at play.
"I'll join your party!" I boldly declared,
But they sped off, leaving me quite scared.

As I sunbathed on the warm, soft sand,
A beach ball rolled and liked my hand.
"Who knew beach life could be so bright?"
With laughter echoing into the night.

Twilight Over a Hidden Cove

The sun dipped down, the night was near,
I asked a crab to lend me an ear.
"What's the secret to cove's delight?"
He blinked at me, then dashed out of sight.

Stars twinkled like disco balls high,
While fish started dancing, oh my, oh my!
"Let's throw a party, it's sunset bliss!"
But a clam just yawned, "I'll pass on this."

The breeze brought giggles, whispers of glee,
As a turtle participated, rather slowly.
"Catch me if you can!" I shouted with glee,
But all I caught was seaweed, oh woe is me.

A jellyfish zapped, breaking the mood,
I slipped on a rock, oh what a crude!
Yet under the stars, laughter still grew,
For every mishap, there's fun waiting too.

The Siren's Invitation

"Come and sing!" the siren did plea,
While I sipped my drink, feeling carefree.
"But wait! I forgot my melody!"
She sighed and rolled her eyes at me.

Fish fins flailed in a glittering trance,
While I tried my best at a silly dance.
The waves laughed so hard, they spilled my drink,
"A fine performer," they chirped, "don't you think?"

"Join our choir, we'll make you a star!"
I waved my hands like a wiggly car.
But when I opened my mouth to sing,
It sounded more like a cat with a string.

The siren chuckled, my notes all askew,
"It's not about talent, just have fun too!"
So we laughed and splashed under evening's glow,
With fish as my chorus, we stole the show.

Beneath the Banyan Shade

In the shade of the banyan tree, oh so grand,
I found a lost flip-flop, not quite as planned.
"You're not my size!" I shouted in fright,
While squirrels giggled, giving me quite the sight.

A wise old turtle peeked from his shell,
"What brings you here? Would you like some gel?"
I blinked, confused, he offered me sunblock,
"Just don't put it on your favorite sock!"

The monkeys swung by with a coconut treat,
"Can you juggle this?" they dared with glee fleet.
I threw up my hands, they all shouted hooray,
But the coconut landed—right on my sleigh.

As laughter echoed through branches and leaves,
The banyan tree danced, teasing the eaves.
With my flip-flops mismatched, I joined in the fun,
For shade and silly games are never quite done.

Journeys in Salty Air

A seagull stole my sandwich,
I shouted, "That's not fair!"
He just squawked in delight,
My lunch flew through the air.

With flip-flops on my feet,
I chased him down the sand,
Instead of tasty bites,
I got sunburned and tanned.

The waves were simply laughing,
As I tried to surf in vain,
Fell face-first in the water,
Thought I'd never walk again.

But here's the quirky lesson,
Life's better with a grin,
For every goofy mishap,
There's a treasure to begin.

Reflections on Crystal Waters

I dived into the ocean,
Thought I'd see a fish or two,
But all I found was seaweed,
And a shoe that's lost its crew.

The turtles held a meeting,
With snacks of jelly beans,
They looked at me all puzzled,
"Who invited this human being?"

The crabs were close to giggling,
As I tried to catch a wave,
But all my splashing antics,
Made them think I'm rather brave.

So if you seek adventure,
In waters deep and wide,
Just bring a sense of humor,
And let the laughter ride.

Island Beneath the Stars

At night the stars are twinkling,
Like a disco ball on high,
I tried to dance with fireflies,
And ended up with a pie.

The moon looked down in wonder,
At my missteps on the beach,
I tripped on all the laughter,
And the shore began to screech.

A crab became my partner,
With his moves, he stole the show,
We spun and slid together,
In a cha-cha with the glow.

So if you find an island,
With stars that blink and twirl,
Join a dance with nature,
And let your worries swirl.

The Heartbeat of the Shore

The shore has its own rhythm,
A heartbeat soft and sweet,
It hums to all the wanderers,
Who shuffle with their feet.

The waves provide the bassline,
That tickles sand below,
While the gulls serve up the vocals,
In the wind they freely flow.

I tried to start a conga,
But fell instead in sand,
The crabs joined in the chorus,
As they clapped with tiny hands.

So follow the shore's tempo,
Dance like crazy with delight,
For every funny moment,
Turns the dark into pure light.

Island Echoes of Time

The sun is out, the crabs do dance,
While tourists lose their flip-flop chance.
Seagulls squawk in harmony,
Stealing chips from you and me.

The waves shout jokes, they're clever, right?
A beachball takes off in flight.
Palm trees laugh at the lazy breeze,
As beach-goers munch their wedged cheese.

Old tales spoke of treasures grand,
But all we found was gooey sand.
Forget the pirates, we'll just loaf,
Sipping coconut milk, that's our oath!

Time drips slow, like melted ice,
With every hiccup, life's real nice.
On this shore, we make our stand,
In laughter's glow, we've struck gold and sand.

Beneath the Mango Canopy

Mangoes drop like comedy skits,
While squirrels plot their cheeky hits.
Under the trees, we share our dreams,
As laughter flows in fruity streams.

With sticky hands, we sip our drinks,
And giggle at the seagulls' winks.
The mango's pit is a treasure chest,
Filled with juice and playful jest.

The lizards skitter, acting bold,
As they tell tales that are pure gold.
In this grove, mischief's our vibe,
As we trade giggles like a bribe.

So let the breeze tickle your face,
In this zany, tropical space.
With every bite of sun-kissed fruit,
We find joy that's not too cute!

Driftwood Tales of Island Dreams

Driftwood gathers like lost requests,
Each piece thinking it knows best.
The beach is a stage, wacky and bright,
Where tides tell tales, day and night.

A crab offers its unsolicited views,
While a starfish snores and refuses to move.
Seashells gossip with soft, salty breath,
Reciting legends of ocean's depth.

With every splash and every fall,
We weave our dreams, we share our call.
A wave crashes down, it's pure mirth,
Who knew sand could bring such worth?

Tanned toes high, we laugh like fools,
With dreams that dance on the ocean's drools.
In driftwood tales, we find our muse,
As laughter echoes in colorful hues.

Beneath the Banyan's Embrace

Beneath the banyan, we gather 'round,
With roots that twist like chaotic sound.
Laughter spills like soda pop,
As shadows play and time won't stop.

Monkeys swing with comic flair,
While we share secrets, without a care.
The breeze is light, jokes fill the air,
As we count leaves and mingle there.

A sage once said, 'A clown's a tree,'
Under this canopy, we agree.
With buzzing bees and snapping twigs,
Our stories tumble like hearty jigs.

So here we sit, with laughter grand,
A merry crew on this silly land.
In the banyan's arms, we truly delight,
Writing our tales until the night.

Cradled by the Coconuts

In a hammock shaped like a giant fruit,
Coconuts chatter like they're in pursuit.
A parrot squawks jokes, the sun's out to play,
Laughter erupts, chasing clouds away.

Bananas join in with a sassy dance,
While turtles on surfboards take a chance.
Oh, the mischief draped in this sunny land,
Where even the breeze seems to have a plan.

The waves are tickling the sandy toes,
As crabs do a shuffle in their funny clothes.
Coconuts giggle, what a silly sight,
In the embrace of day, everything feels right.

Here fun grows wild, like vines on a tree,
Each moment a laugh, oh, so carefree.
With nature's humor, the night starts to bloom,
And the stars wink, echoing all the room.

Beneath the Tidal Moon

The moon is a lamp with its glow all askew,
While jellyfish waltz in their gelatin crew.
Shells play the drums as the tides roll and twist,
Calling the fish to join in the tryst.

With surfboards and laughter, the fish take a spin,
Mermaids host parties, bringing the whim.
Octopuses juggle with tentacles wide,
While sea turtles show off their dance on the tide.

Glowworms pop up, giving shine to the night,
And seaweed sways to a catchy delight.
Here, the ocean pockets its secrets and shade,
As crabs try to swing, but their plans often fade.

Under the stars, all the critters unite,
Creating a beach bash, a comical sight.
The moon grins down, it's a watery trance,
As waves giggle waves in a fanciful dance.

Forgotten Footprints in the Sand

Footprints in the sand tell tales of the clumsy,
Some zigzag like lost, others look lumbery.
Flip-flops flew off, in a mad dash to flee,
While seashells just chuckle, "Come try to catch me!"

Sunburned noses and hats askew,
Sandy sandwiches, with half-eaten stew.
Waves that come rolling with laughter of their own,
Covering secrets that the beach has known.

Here comes a seagull, diving for crumbs,
In a fierce battle for snacks, oh the bums!
Coconut drinks spill like a party gone wild,
As children roll laughing, each moment beguiled.

The sun sets softly, painting gold on the shore,
As tired feet wander, but still want some more.
Among the footprints, adventures unfold,
As memories linger, like seashells of gold.

A Canvas of Stars Above

The stars are a canvas, splashed with bright fun,
Like cosmic confetti, all twinkling and spun.
A shooting star trips, steals the show with a laugh,
Making wishes tumble like a magical craft.

Fireflies blink, sharing secrets with glee,
While a crab in a tux dreams of dancing free.
The moon giggles softly, winks at the crowd,
As the waves tap the shore, feeling joyful and proud.

Clouds fluff like pillows, floating through space,
While the night wears a blanket of lacy embrace.
And jokes of the universe ripple through air,
Tickling the night with mischief to share.

All beings are welcome in this nighttime party,
Where shadows do cha-chas and nothing feels hearty.
Beneath the wide heavens, with laughter unbound,
Each twinkle a memory; joy knows no ground.

Legends of the Fading Horizon

Once a crab wore a fancy hat,
He danced on the shore, sleek as a cat.
Seagulls laughed, wings spread wide,
He thought he was quite the seaside pride.

A dolphin made waves, gliding in high,
With a joke about fish that flew in the sky.
But the fish, looking up, gave a wink,
Which made the ocean giggle and sink.

A turtle played chess with a clam,
To see who could yield the better jam.
'Checkmate!' cried the clam, with his shell all aglow,
But the turtle just said, 'Now, where's my slow-mo?'

So legends grow where the seagulls play,
In sunny old shores that brighten the day.
With hats, dolphins' pranks, and a turtle's spree,
This funny isle holds a magic, you see!

Currents of Serenity and Solitude

A pufferfish puffed, then giggled aloud,
Swam off with a splash, feeling quite proud.
But the stingray sighed, saying, 'Not so fast!'
'You'll float away far, caught up in your blast!'

A hermit crab settled in a bright shoe,
Claimed it was vintage, 'Most stylish too!'
A crabby old crab said, 'That's not your size!'
'Oh shush!' said the hermit, 'It's all about vibes!'

A lone octopus looked for a friend,
Tricked a poor shrimp, to the pool he did send.
'Join me for salsa!' he said with a wink,
The shrimp did the tango, oh what a blink!

On waves of fun, they all twirled and swayed,
In currents of joy, their worries delayed.
Where solitude sparkled with humor profound,
Laughter echoed in depths where love could be found!

Whispers of the Tides

A crab on the beach wrote tales in the sand,
With a feathered quill tucked under his hand.
He whispered to waves, 'Oh won't you come near?'
The tide laughed and answered, 'My dear, don't you fear!'

A starfish told secrets to shells on the shore,
About pirates and treasures - oh, what a score!
Seashells listened close, with wide-open grins,
As the seabreeze chimed in with snickers and spins.

A horse in the surf tried to gallop with grace,
But tumbled and rolled, filled with foam on his face.
The fish all burst forth in hysterical fits,
While the horse laughed along, 'Oh, I love making hits!'

So whispers emerge from the depths of the sea,
Where laughter rings out, forever carefree.
In tides that exchange every giggle and sigh,
It's fun and mischief where the seabirds fly!

Echoes Beneath the Palm

Beneath the tall palm, a lizard crooned,
Sipping on coconut, feeling immune.
A monkey swung down, tail all a tease,
'Careful, you don't want to spill that, please!'

A parrot cawed jokes about sailors' might,
'They never find treasure enough for a bite!'
But the lizard just laughed, saying, 'I'm full of delight,
A nut from the palm makes the wrongs all feel right!'

A turtle strolled by, in glasses so round,
He chuckled at passersby with a sound.
'In my slow and stylish, I take such a drag,'
The others all giggled, 'You've got quite a wag!'

So beneath every palm, tales twist and twirl,
Of creatures and quirks in a whirl of a swirl.
With laughter and fun brewing round every bend,
The echoes of joy shine bright, my dear friend!

A Mosaic of Ocean Memories

In the sun, the crabs do dance,
With little shoes, they prance.
Fish wear hats, oh what a sight,
As waves giggle, morning light.

Seagulls squawk in silly tunes,
While dolphins juggle with bright moons.
The sandcastles aim so high,
But crumble down with a shy sigh.

Turtles in shades, they cruise the shore,
Each wave is a knock, they want to explore.
Shells laugh softly, whispering lore,
In this ocean, who could want more?

As sunset fades, they say, "Oh dear!"
"Tomorrow's antics will appear!"
With a wink, the sea will tease,
And we'll join in with joyful ease.

Whispered Odes of the Winds

The breeze is gossiping, quick and sly,
It tickles noses, makes laughter fly.
Kites take off, looking so grand,
While kids tumble, not quite as planned.

Banana boats bump, hardly afloat,
Giggling as they turn into a boat.
The wind shouts secrets, soft and light,
As gulls play tag, taking their flight.

Flip-flops squeak in a crazed ballet,
Echoing hues of a sunny day.
The waves insist, "We're here for fun!"
While umbrellas shade, two legs run.

As dusk brings calm, the sails still sway,
The whispers of the winds, here to stay.
With a sprinkle of stars, the beach feels right,
Together we laugh, under the night.

Tides of Ancients and New Beginnings

Sand and shells hold tales untold,
Of mermaids, pirates, adventures bold.
But here comes Tommy, with a water gun,
Declaring, "Water wars are so much fun!"

Old logs lie like giants asleep,
While children build where secrets keep.
The tide rolls in, with its chilly bite,
Yet everyone jumps in, what a sight!

Moonlit dances on the soft sand,
With goofy moves that look so planned.
The tide gives us a playful shove,
As laughter echoes, it's just pure love.

As stars twinkle above with glee,
"More fun adventures, just you and me!"
And as the ocean whispers past,
We vow these moments will forever last.

Tranquil Portals to Reveries

The hammock swings, a gentle sway,
A portal to dreams, come out to play.
With ice cream cones, so drippy and sweet,
While crabs juggle, our laughter's the beat.

Colors of sunset, flaming and grand,
They tiptoe with joy across the sand.
Each wave that crashes tells a bright tale,
Of silly fish and a floppy whale.

Beach ball season, the rules unclear,
Who threw it first? We all just cheer!
Sandy toes and sun-kissed cheeks,
In this paradise, laughter peaks.

As night unfolds, the stars ignite,
Frogs serenade under the moonlight.
The ocean hums, with a cozy tune,
"Stay forever, under the silver moon."

Nature's Cryptic Messages

A squirrel with a secret grin,
Whispers to the lizard kin.
The flowers giggle, tickle-breeze,
While turtles play, with utmost ease.

A tree stump laughs at passing ants,
Who lost their way, forgot their dance.
The wind writes jokes in rustling leaves,
As sunlight winks and gently teases.

A cheeky crab with a sideways strut,
Claims every puddle is his hut.
The fish flip-flop in silly shows,
While frogs croak tunes, nobody knows.

Mice in hats form a ballet line,
Practicing for dinner's wine.
Nature's stage is wild and bright,
With every creature's laughter, delight.

Calligraphy of the Ocean's Breath

Waves curl like a poet's pen,
Writing stories now and then.
Seagulls cackle from above,
Chasing dreams and fish they love.

Salty air makes hair go wild,
A crab declared a king, beguiled.
Octopuses in a dance-off sway,
Splashing ink in a jazzy way.

The sun does salsa on the tide,
As jellyfish take a joyful ride.
Shells gossip like old chums anew,
Each tide brings gossip, bubbly brew.

Beachcomber's hat flies off his head,
As gulls conspire, just like they said.
On this canvas, laughter flows,
With each wave, hilarity grows!

Palm Leaves and Moonlight

Under palms that sway and tease,
The moon peeks down, quite at ease.
A party of shadows plays around,
With giggles and whispers all abound.

Night crickets cheer, a symphony great,
While raccoons plan a midnight fate.
Stars wink at stories untold,
As fireflies dress in glittering gold.

Coconuts debate who's the best,
While owls compete in fashion zest.
The sea sings soft lullabies sweet,
As laughter echoes on every beat.

Palm leaves rustle in silly chats,
Scaring chums like playful cats.
In the moonlight, fun finds its way,
A nightly talescape, come what may!

Veil of Mist Over Shimmering Waters

A misty veil drapes the shore,
Where dolphins play and splish, they score.
They challenge waves with bubbly grins,
As seahorses twirl and spin.

The fog wears laughter like a cloak,
Seagulls dance, joking with a yoke.
Sand dollars chuckle deep in the sand,
All part of a vacation grand.

Fish hold comedy night at bay,
Cracking jokes with every sway.
Eels in stripes, they shimmy and slide,
While turtles giggle on their ride.

The sun peeks through, a playful tease,
As clams tell tales of "Oh, please!"
In this misty realm, fun prevails,
Where laughter's carried on gentle gales.

Coves of Memory and Longing

In the cove where memories play,
Old sandals are lost, washed away.
Seagulls squawk a curious tune,
Chasing the sun, oh, what a boon!

Crab competes in a racing dash,
With a determined, cheeky splash.
We sit and laugh, a sandy throne,
Sharing stories, enchanted, alone.

Old friends poke fun at the tide,
Claiming they're wise, but it's a ride.
Each wave brings a fresh surprise,
And flip-flops flying through the skies!

The memories dance on salty breeze,
Carried along with utmost ease.
In these coves, we're never old,
Just beach bums with tales to be told.

Breezes that Carry Hidden Stories

Whispers swirl like a beach ball,
Tales of sandcastles, big and small.
The breeze giggles, tickles our ears,
As it gathers our laughter and cheers.

A mermaid swims by with a wink,
Her sarcasm drips with salty ink.
Shells giggle, wearing their bright hats,
While octopuses make silly spats.

Coconut drinks with tiny umbrellas,
Hide behind jokes from quirky fellas.
Every gust, a cocoon of wit,
As the sun starts to lose its grit.

Stories mingle in twilight's grace,
As dusk blushes and lights up space.
The waves laugh too; they flap and clap,
In this breeze of fun, we all unwrap.

Shores that Call to the Wanderer

Footprints in sand leave tales untold,
Wanderer grins, bold and old.
A seagull squawks, joins the parade,
Mixing laughter with the sun's cascade.

Sneaky crabs plot their next great feat,
Pinching toes, they can't be beat!
The wanderer dances with glee,
In a haphazard two-step spree.

Old shells whisper secrets of the past,
With sandy jokes that always last.
The tide rolls in, plays its card,
Good vibes swimming; it's never hard.

As sun dips low, we share our dreams,
Knocking over ice cream, or so it seems.
In this dance where spirits intertwine,
We are young and foolish, forever divine.

Shores of Light and Shadow

Shores where shadows make a fuss,
Stumbling over jellyfish—what a plus!
Flip-flops squeak, our laughter loud,
As footprints fade beneath the shroud.

The sun plays tricks, a peek-a-boo,
While we sip drinks, our minds adieu.
Pirates pass with jests so grand,
Searching for treasure, not quite planned.

Umbrellas tilt like hats in a dance,
While folks attempt to balance in chance.
Shadow puppets offer their lore,
Creating giggles, and nothing more.

As light winks, and shadows retreat,
The night rolls in with a calm heartbeat.
In this dance of chaos and cheer,
We find that happiness is always near.

Serenade of the Seagulls

Seagulls laugh with glee, oh, what a sight,
Chasing chips that fly out, such pure delight.
With wings like flappers, they dance in the breeze,
Screeching songs of joy, fluttering with ease.

On the sandy stage, they strut with flair,
Snatching snacks from toddlers who simply stare.
A feathery chorus in the warm, bright day,
Hoping for a morsel, come what may.

As waves roll along, they wiggle and dip,
Spinning sandy tales with a salty flip.
In a world of bikinis, they rule with a laugh,
In this coastal symphony, they're the epitaph.

So next time you wander down by the shore,
Listen to their antics, you'll surely want more.
With wild, rattling calls and a sense of play,
Seagulls sing their serenade, come join the fray.

Treasures in the Driftwood

Driftwood art pieces washed upon the sand,
A chair, a table, or a weary hand.
Each twist and turn tells of stories untold,
Treasures of the sea, slowly bought, slowly sold.

Some pieces are wobbly, like those on a spree,
Pretending to be furniture, don't you see?
But with a bit of paint and a quirky charm,
They'll grace your backyard, offering no harm.

But beware of the knots, they come with a tale,
Whispers of sailors lost in a gale.
If you listen closely, you might hear them say,
"Don't build a ship from wood on a sunny day!"

So gather your finds, let your laughter ring,
With driftwood treasures, create everything.
From quirky to odd, let your dreams take flight,
In driftwood's embrace, the world's a delight.

Where Waves Might Whisper

Waves roll in softly, speaking through foam,
As I sit and ponder, away from my home.
They bubble and giggle, a secret to tell,
Of fishy affairs and the ocean's own spell.

Little crabs wearing spectacles scuttle around,
Racing past sandcastles that tumble down.
They chuckle and wink, with a pinch and a glare,
In this raucous ocean, life's never unfair.

Sea stars lounge lazily, sipping sea tea,
Complaining of the shells, too salty to be.
With laughter, they roll, in a parade of delight,
Under the moon's glow, all seems just right.

So next time you wander where echoes reside,
Join in the fun, on the salty tide.
Listen for the waves, they know how to tease,
In the whispers of surf, you'll find all that frees.

Elysium of Sunlit Greens

In an island garden, so bright and so bold,
The veggies are gossiping, tales are retold.
A cucumber and tomato, both sporting a grin,
Debating who's juicier, let the games begin!

Sunflowers are swaying, strutting their stuff,
Bidding on the bees, "Hey, we're sweet enough!"
With petals like crowns, they reign over the patch,
In this verdant kingdom, no seedling to scratch.

A dandelion puffs in a haughty boast,
"I'm the real weed king; I thrive the most!"
While carrots hide under, they're quite shy and meek,
Craving a spotlight, just a day of chic.

So revel in greens, where laughter is free,
In the sunshine's embrace, come sip on your tea.
For in this garden haven, where joy is supreme,
Every leaf takes a bow, living life like a dream.

A Florid Elixír of Nature

In a garden where giggles bloom,
Sunflowers wear hats like a shampoo.
Bees dance cha-cha in the sweet air,
While rabbits play poker without a care.

The daisies debate if they're lovely or not,
And tulips gossip about that silly pot.
But watch out for snails, they're sneaky and sly,
With a plan to steal lettuce—oh my, oh my!

Each breeze brings a tickle, a whimsical jest,
Even pumpkins laugh, feeling quite blessed.
Nature's a jester, no frown in sight,
In this florid realm, everything's light.

So here's to the world with its comical twist,
Where flowers wear crowns and nothing is missed.
Let's sip on this laughter, our favorite brew,
For joy is the best—who needs a shoe?

Dreams on the Ocean's Breath

The waves whispered secrets from faraway places,
They tickled the toes of sunburned faces.
Seagulls squawk tales of a fish named Fred,
Who wore a top hat—it's what we all said.

A crab with a monocle snapped at the tide,
While fish played marbles, their scales open wide.
Mermaids were singing, or so it appeared,
They harmonized hiccups, making us cheered.

Underwater parties where bubbles do dance,
A turtle in shades gives each fish a chance.
With laughter like echoes from beneath the blue,
Life's a grand jest, with a seaweed review.

So grab your floaties and join in the fun,
In dreams where the ocean outshines the sun.
With every wave crashing, let giggles arise,
As splashes of joy fill our hearts and our skies.

Shadows Beneath the Almond Tree

Underneath the almond, where shade bounces light,
A squirrel's upending a picnic delight.
Chips on his paws and a sandwich in tow,
He nibbles and prances, a nutty grande show.

The ants form a conga, all marching in line,
To the beat of a beetle's sweet tambourine rhyme.
While a lizard in shades critiques every move,
He's the judge in this contest, with a cool groove.

A rabbit, quite certain he's king of the hill,
Transforms into jokes with an acorn to spill.
He tells all the critters, "Here's the scoop, hoot!
Let's party tonight—it's a nutty pursuit!"

As shadows stretch longer, the antics unfold,
Beneath the almond tree, laughter is bold.
With each passing day, we find jests so quaint,
In the land of the nuts, every creature's a saint.

A Symphony of Seafoam

The ocean's a conductor, waves rise and fall,
Shells play the violins while seagulls enthrall.
A crab on the flute makes a jazzy good tune,
As dolphins do pirouettes, all under the moon.

Foamy mischief bubbles with a giggly sigh,
Tickling the sand as the sea breezes fly.
A clam sings a ballad, though flat as can be,
The octopus twirls with glee, don't you see?

The chorus of laughter will echo tonight,
Where jellyfish glow with a shimmering light.
Each splash is a note, each ripple a line,
In this symphony crafted by nature divine.

So let's join the concert, both silly and free,
With sandcastles rising like musical spree.
In the symphony of seafoam, where fun's the refrain,
We dance to the rhythms, again and again.

Shores of Forgotten Dreams

A crab in a bowtie stole my lunch,
It danced on the shore with a silly crunch.
Seagulls squawked like they owned the place,
While I tried to keep up with the frantic pace.

Flip-flops went flying, what a sight!
Well, there goes my left shoe, oh what a fright.
The ocean waves giggled, tickling my toes,
As jellyfish wiggled in their fancy prose.

Sandcastles crumbled, oh my, what a shame!
A pirate appeared, though he looked pretty tame.
He offered me treasure, but all that I found,
Were socks filled with shells, all littered around.

With sun on my skin and wind in my hair,
I laughed at the antics of seaweed's lair.
Life on the shore is a whimsical dream,
Where laughter and mischief reign supreme.

Secrets of the Coral Reef

Bubbles burble secrets from fish so spry,
They giggle and wiggle as they swim on by.
A turtle in glasses reads the ocean's news,
While octopuses juggle in bright polka shoes.

The clams are all gossiping, whispering fast,
About a mermaid with a party to blast.
She invites the whole reef, oh what a delight,
With seaweed confetti and lights shiny bright.

But wait! The clownfish is stealing the show,
With jokes that could make even dolphins go 'whoa!'
They laugh and they splash, a comical scene,
Amidst coral castles, all painted in green.

Underwater shenanigans, all around me,
Life's a big circus, oh can't you see?
In this coral playground, we dance and we play,
Where every silly moment makes brighter the day.

A Lure from the Horizon

A sailboat sailed in with a quirky crew,
They wore mismatched socks and hats, too askew.
With a parrot that squawked, 'What's on the menu?'
They laughed as they dined on spaghetti and stew.

The sun set low, painting skies all aglow,
A disco ball rose, with a shimmering show.
Dancing coconuts joined in the fun,
Twisting and swaying till the night was done.

A treasure map drawn in peanut butter spread,
Led us to snacks and a meal of pure bread.
But the real treasure was laughter and cheer,
As we toasted with pineapples and sipped on root beer.

With dreams like these, who needs gold or jewels?
When good times are found with the ocean's fools.
So let the horizon forever inspire,
A life filled with giggles and endless desire.

Song of the Wind-Washed Sands

The wind whistled songs to the grains on the shore,
As I built up my castle, but it fell once more.
A seagull swooped down, of sandwich a thief,
Eating my lunch while I stared in disbelief.

The tides twinkled rhythmic, a beach ball parade,
As shells joined the dance in the sun's warm cascade.
The sand tickled toes, a soft playful tease,
While a crab squeezed my leg - oh, give me some ease!

Bikini-clad beings sunbathed with flair,
While I tried to blend in, but couldn't quite dare.
Then laughter erupted, led by a child,
Whose sand sculpting skills left the beach quite wild.

With buckets of joy and spades of delight,
We all joined together to laugh into night.
For the song of the sands is a whimsical tune,
Where fun finds a way to make every heart swoon.

Whispers of Distant Shores

The sea breeze danced with laughter loud,
Seagulls snickered, mischief unbowed.
Crabs in suits, with top hats worn,
Belched out jokes, we're never forlorn.

Beach balls bounced with glee in tow,
Sunburnt folks, all in a row.
Flip-flops flapping, a silly parade,
Chasing ice cream, under the shade.

Sandcastles built to noble height,
Only to splash in waves of delight.
Mermen invited, but forgot the snacks,
Now they've got a seaweed knick-knack!

With laughter echoing off the sand,
The ocean shared its tickling hand.
Under the sun, joy didn't cease,
For every wave brought giggles and peace.

Echoes Beneath the Palms

Palm trees swayed like they knew a joke,
Falling coconuts, a jester's poke.
Swinging hammocks, where dreams collide,
With hiccuping waves, they laughed and sighed.

The sun, a joker with shades so bright,
Painted the sky for a colorful fight.
Laughter bubbled from fish in the sea,
While dolphins danced, as happy as can be.

Bikini-clad friends, a sight to behold,
Fell face-first in sand, a tale to be told.
Waves crashing, a rhythmic cheer,
While sunburned faces grinned ear to ear.

Echoes of giggles bounced through the palm,
Every flip of a flop, a comic balm.
This paradise, where the funny resides,
Turns everyday woes into joyful tides.

Lure of the Sun-Kissed Horizon

The horizon winked, a cheeky greet,
As surfboards sneezed, the landing fleet.
Waves rolled in, with a roaring laugh,
Tickling toes on their sandy path.

Cocktails clinked like friends in glee,
With umbrellas bright, as silly as can be.
Sipping laughter, hiccuped delight,
As sunburns turned into a funny sight.

Seashells whispered secrets of old,
Like gossiping friends, daring and bold.
Jumping jellies in a jiggy dance,
Made everyone giggle, a joyful chance.

As the sun dipped low, casting tones of gold,
The beach embraced tales yet untold.
With warmth in our hearts and laughter aligned,
We chased the horizon, funny and kind.

Secrets of the Tide-Embraced Land

Tide pools giggled with starfish delight,
While crabs donned crowns, ready for night.
Seashells clattered, a musical show,
As seaweed wiggled, dancing below.

The beachcombers trotted, finding their fate,
Tripping on flip-flops, oh, isn't it great?
With treasure maps scribbled in ink of a pen,
X marks where laughter shall happen again!

Breezes teased the surfers on shore,
Who wiped out in style, leaving us wanting more.
With salty tongues and sunburnt cheeks,
They recounted their tales, as the sunset peaks.

In this land embraced by salt and cheer,
Every wave promised laughter around here.
Secrets lie waiting, like whispers in sand,
Unraveling humor, a treasure so grand.

Mysteries of the Distant Isle

There's a crab wearing shades in the sun,
Strutting on sand, oh what fun!
Seagulls gossip in feathery rows,
While a turtle practices its slow-motion shows.

The coconuts laugh in the palm tree's sway,
Sharing secrets of last night's fray.
A fish in a tux, so dapper and neat,
Winks at a mermaid, oh what a treat!

Shells act like phones, all buzzing with cheer,
'Come for a swim, the coast is clear!'
The waves bring tales from far and wide,
As the island giggles with cheerful pride.

With each sunset, the sand jokes anew,
Puns and jests from surf to dew.
The distant isle beckons with laughter so bold,
Where adventures await, both silly and gold.

Twilight's Dance with the Sea

In twilight's glow, the waves start to prance,
The fish have a party, let's join the dance!
With seaweed tassels, they sway and they twirl,
Even the clam shell gives a silly whirl.

Seagulls wear hats made of foam and of light,
They caw out puns under the stars of the night.
A dolphin does leaping, a show of its glee,
While the barnacles clap, 'What a sight to see!'

Moonbeams bring laughter, soft ripples of fun,
Crabs with their banter, a comedy run.
With bubbles and laughter, the shoreline is bright,
In the dance of the twilight, all is just right.

While shadows grow longer, and stars start to wink,
The ocean is telling a joke, don't you think?
As the laughter lingers, the night knows no end,
Where every wet whimsy is sure to suspend.

Sundrenched Soliloquy

Sunshine giggles on the warm, golden sand,
While kids have a barbecue, grilling on demand.
The skies wear their bluest, a canvas so grand,
With a floaty in the pool, I'm trying to stand!

A hermit crab hosts the best sandy soirée,
Inviting all guests for a beachy buffet.
A pineapple sings, with its fruity allure,
'Please pass the marshmallows, I'm not quite sure!'

Flip-flops argue about who's more fly,
While surfboards debate if they can glide high.
The ice-cream cone slowly melts in the heat,
A piano made of seashells plays a jazzy beat.

As sunlight dips low, and shadows grow long,
The sea whisper-shouts its own silly song.
In this sundrenched haven where humor ignites,
Every grain of sand knows the joy of delights.

Lighthouses of Longing

A lighthouse winks with its bright, beaming eye,
'Come closer, you sailors, don't be shy!'
Its light dances quick, like a flirt on a spree,
While seagulls sing ballads, oh so carefree.

The boats in the harbor have stories to tell,
Of storms and of calm, of missing the swell.
With fish in their nets, they knit tales of glee,
While the lighthouse chuckles, 'Who needs a decree?'

Each wave is a whisper, each tide brings a grin,
With sunsets that sparkle, where laughter can win.
The dockhands are jesters with ropes in their hand,
As they trip on their laces, a comedic stand.

So here at the edge of the world and the sea,
Where longing meets laughter, we're ever so free.
Under the starlit sky, we'll dance to its song,
In this whimsical haven, we all do belong.

Hidden Paths to Paradise

Around the bend, with flip-flops sound,
A squirrel laughs as he's found,
Tropical drinks spill as we trip,
Who knew the jungle would be a skip?

With coconuts falling, oh what a flare,
The parrot squawks in a funky air,
We dance by the waves with hair askew,
Is that a crab or just a shoe?

Mismatched socks are the perfect flair,
A treasure map on a picnic chair,
Pirate dreams with a burger side,
Wandering those paths of joy and pride.

With laughter echoing through the sky,
Each step taken makes me sigh,
Who knew paradise had such glee?
With friends like these, I'm so carefree!

From Dunes to Whispered Dreams

In the sand, we make a fort,
Sandy snacks? Now that's a sport!
Using shells as our spoons and cups,
Where the tide rolls in, our laughter erupts.

Seagulls cackle, they join the fun,
Chasing each other, oh how they run!
Beach balls bounce off each head,
The sun's hot, but we won't be wed.

From dunes we slide, with giggles galore,
Each tumble down calls for one encore,
As laughter echoes, we can't believe,
This day of dreams, we won't deceive!

With lemonade and sandy toes,
Life's best moments, who really knows?
From sunny shores to the twilight beam,
What a joy to live this dream!

Castaway's Serenade to the Sea

Stranded here with mango trees,
Join me friend, let's catch some breeze,
The island's quiet, a gentle tease,
Or was that a shark? Just a tease!

With a ukulele made of driftwood,
I strum a tune, hoping it's good,
A pufferfish swims by, does he care?
Or is he laughing at my wild hair?

A message in a bottle, oh what's this?
Just a note saying 'make a wish',
A crab joins in for the night's serenade,
As the moonlight glimmers, memories are made.

With coconuts cracking like jokes all night,
The stars above seem to twinkle in delight,
Though I may never escape this spree,
I've found my joy in the open sea!

Lighthouses of Longing and Light

Oh lighthouse keeper, what's the key?
To find the humor in the sea?
With beams so bright, he twirls around,
His only audience is the crabs on the ground.

Seagulls squawk in tune so loud,
Each wave crashes in a funny shroud,
We tip the boat, oh what a sight,
Laughter rising with each moonlight.

In the lantern's glow, stories unfold,
Tales of seafarers brave and bold,
But they trip over nets and fish that bite,
Who knew the sea was such a fright?

With the lighthouse waving like it's dancing,
Each glimmer brings a smile, enhancing,
In this port where laughter ignites,
The light of joy shines through the nights.

www.ingramcontent.com/pod-product-compliance
Lightning Source LLC
Chambersburg PA
CBHW072129070526
44585CB00016B/1600